Memory Outside The Head

John Grey

CONTENTS

WHAT SETS US OFF

Dogs bark at one a.m.
Nothing out there.
No reason I can see
for them to get riled up,
eyes blazing,
hair raised.

As far as they're concerned,
something intruded on their space
which is, according to their instincts,
my territory as well.

Maybe the radiator spooked them.
Or a floor-board creaked.
Or a car backfired.
Or a mouse scurried somewhere
within the walls.

Their minds can fashion
a threatening monster
from the merest of sounds.

I calm them down,
slip back into bed,
fall asleep.

A flicker of memory,
a modicum of mood,
a smidgen of stress,
my dreams get down
to being dogs.

ON OUR LAST NIGHT TOGETHER, SHE TOLD ME THIS

She's telling me what would happen
if the sun went out
just like this camp-fire.

There'd be layers of extinction
with human life somewhere
in the middle.
The plants would go first,
then the animals that eat the plants,
then the ones who eat the animals.
And last, the ones who eat those ones.

She's the champion of
what I never want to hear.
She cuddles close.
For eight minutes everything
would be the same, she says,
because that's how long it takes
for light to get here.

Of course, the air would
gradually cool.
She's talking with her
warm hands by this.
The planets would flick off
in succession like Christmas bulbs in January.

Each kiss represents
the stars, now brighter
in the sky for lack of competition.
Each speculation
wipes her moisture from my cheek.

Of course, there'd still
be heat from the earth's interior.
She stares at my chest
as she says this.
But after a long pause,
she adds...that wouldn't be enough.

There'd be a stillness
like you could never imagine.
No winds, no waves.
The world would be
like your bedroom at night.
The ocean like the cold sheets'
you sink your face into.
COLORADO, MAY 1993

Spanish Peaks jut out of the Great Plains,
abrupt and haughty.
Great volcanic dikes and cockeyed ridges
scorn my eyes.
Ponderosa pine and Alpine fir
cling to the sides,
desperate, wind-gutted.
These mountains do not rise like love,
gentle and sloping,
kissed by oak brush and gently turning aspen.
They leap furiously out of the sameness

like desire,
tough and cloud shredding,
piercing the blue with shaved pointy skulls.
These mountains sate themselves on my staring.
Once they've had enough,
they turn on me with darkness.
If mountains could move on, they would be these,
rough, unstable betrayers of my awe,
vast, unassailable in their treason.

ODD HABITS

Sure I had odd habits.
I snared tadpoles,
kept them in glass jars.
The moment they started growing flippers
and their heads increased in size,
I set them free.
Then I wondered what they thought of me.
Was I the god of those tiny swiveling creatures?
Did my eye peering at them through glass
override all instinct?
And what did the mature frogs
tell the ones that didn't matriculate
through my university of dirty water?
I interfered…actually I prefer interceded
in that amphibian world.
Did my frogs come out different?
More cognizant of their surroundings?
Maybe the slightest bit human by association?
Yes, I had odd habits.
Collecting tadpoles wasn't one of them.
Pretending I shaped destinies was.

IN THE HOUR BEFORE SUNSET

Nerves trembling like pond surface,
in a meadow that's a wide plaza of green,
and above - glorious - the serene blue,
Armand and I race our hearts
from the horizon's pale orange grin
to a den of white poplars on the hill.

We climb the old stone fences,
chant the names on the abandoned graveyard markers,
sweep through a grove of ferns,
windier than wind.
That's the way of the young -
giggle, flutter and yet stay alert
for the gold and black butterfly on a twig,
the squirrel foraging in gold's last drops.

As religious as we can manage
is a stuttered paean to Mother Earth,
where she lies in her gravel,
before oak cross and crow angel,
as below, her children,
sprout first apples in the orchards,
needles in a bevy of pines.

It's all for amusement of two boy-virgins,
brown skin, green eyes, lean of body
and careless with it.
Much growing, much maturing to be done,
say the stay-at-home voices.
But for the rest of life,
today will do nicely.

A MAN OF SECRETS

I've no idea what he is thinking.
And he's not about to tell me;

that's not how it works.
There is a past in there somewhere

but the face is having none of it.
It's too calm for a start,

almost in a state of euphoria.
Nothing fazes a dead man.

Not the rescue, come too late.
Not the cops.

Not the doctor, poking and prodding
to see how long he's been in the water

as if the time he died
has more to say about the man

than the time he lived.
And not the onlookers,

some in shock,
others feeling the guilt

of their ghoulish curiosity.
So it's a relief to know

there's at least one here
who's enjoying himself.

PSYCHIATRISTS AT A PARTY

Some distinguished looking types here;
you're wondering, are any of these people psychiatrists -
small talk tamping a hard day's sessions
with the confused, the angry, the depressed, the beleaguered.

Then you're thinking, do those sessions stop
when the last patient's shown the door
or is each encounter an assessment?
Every conversation, a case history,
even without the prescription, the fee?

The talking is incessant,
so who is more ear than mouth,
perking up like a rabbit
at what's being said three groups away?

Hors d'oeuvres
are being passed around -
watch the most practiced hand,
the one that can grab and swallow
without letting another's spoken word drop.
Who's been trained
by all those *Pfizer* and *Eli Lilly* seminars?

Is there someone here
who can prevent a suicide?
Soothe a frazzled mind
or simply give a troubled tongue
the space to flap?

You're here to enjoy yourself.

It's just you really need to know why.

REPORTING TO THE FISHBOWL

From deep within the fish bowl,
something orange
silently gestures.

A bare bulb above
shines down on my curiosity,
the fish's dire needs.

Everything else in the house
is where it should be,
acting like it must.

Rooms spread away from me
but the floor, the ceiling,
hold their place.

Same with the table
on which the bowl is perched,
and the castle, the rocks within.

The toilet, the sink, refrigerator,
are content for now,
want nothing of me.

It's the fish that calls me out,
its movement that attracts me,
its expression, its interaction.

Life at fishbowl's edge
is communication's last stand.
The poor dumb creature

wishes to be fed.
Or it wants me to know
it's not a poor dumb creature.

THE CIRCUS WAS IN TOWN

I don't remember the performing elephants fondly.
I've worried too much, down the years,
as to the hardship, the unnaturalness,
of their offstage lives.
Same with lions and tigers.
As a boy, I felt the threat to the tamer
with the whip.
Now, my memories take the side
of the big cats.

The food, greasy as it may have been,
was a treasure.
But not so much the clowns.
With other children around,
they were funny.
But, one on one,
they were as scary as headmasters.

But the pretty girls
are what the circus has come down to.
Hardened by the life no doubt
but still fine and fair,
even behind the makeup.

Some stood atop white stallions,
proudly circled the main ring of the Big Top.
Others, in spangling costumes,
floated through the air
from bar to bar

or walked slowly, daringly, across tightropes.
One even hung from a rope
by her teeth.

I went year after year
and the audience dwindled each time.
Now there's only me.
The light from the circus train
has long dimmed over the horizon.
But a blue-eyed blonde is
swinging from the rafters.
There's a net below.
But only as long as I'm living.

A PHANTOM VISIT

A gold moon paves the way.
A red window leads to a blue bed.
Among other things, there is
a phantom in the room
who beguiles the restless child
with arms of smoke
and spidery legs
and a murmur that encircles the room.

The boy is sustained, not terrified.
He is illuminated, set free.
Should the ghost leave,
he will go with him,
follow the fleshless, bloodless imago
through the opening
in this dreadful existence.

For isn't life all hammering fists
in the guise of honey?
And whose eyes glow beguilingly
like this new mentor?
The specter shrinks down
into a beckoning finger
and summoning chants ooze from the walls
like escaping steam.

He's tried other exits.
But books aren't a good enough escape route.
His imagination's sky

lathers up with clouds.
No oak can grow in such a bitter grove.
Let them come upon the empty sheets
and wonder.

He longs for a world
of soft and sure footing,
sterilized of desperation.
If he has to unbind the soul,
then so be it.

But then the interloper fades.
The room is just a room.
Reality's cold shadow creeps across his face.
Black tears gather on his cheeks like ravens.

VILLAGE LIFE

Running bathwater on one side,
Miles Davis on the other,
above, the wannabe diva
screeching something from Turandot,
in my one room and half-kitchen,
a small black and white TV,
a pawn shop guitar,
a purring ginger cat,
another neighbor in my one chair
drinking my last beer,
complaining how he can't get a job,
down below, the small falafel shop
squeezed with hungry dancers, artists,
on the sidewalk, a street musician
strumming the poor up for change,
a junkie crashed on a stoop,
the local whore grocery shopping
or is that the local grocery shopper whoring,
and all in the name of
life experience, required research -
on the table, a second hand typewriter,
a blank sheet of paper,
awaiting the payoff.

IN SEARCH OF EDGAR ALLAN POE

This August night, the drizzle is a kind
of sunshine, soft and reliable,
soothing cool against the face.
It softly thrums my cheekbones as I stroll

Benefit Street's lumpen sidewalks.
I find Poe prints but no Poe.
The moon's a thin one.
The light is sporadic and watery.

It's evening and something flies overhead.
A raven? More likely a bat.
They're out to make a living.
I seek kinship with the past.

Any one of these stoops
could have been Poe's courting place.
Or the doorway
he turned away from in despair.

My imagination is bait
for any shape or sound.
Was that the crackle of Sarah Whitman's petticoats?
Or just wind blowing last year's leaves around?

A plaque on a wall reads 1848.
A window's lit with candles.
A tree, old and gnarly,
is rooted in broken brick.

I find Poe prints but no Poe.
Then a mist rises up
from stark, morose masonry.
I swear it's blowing my way.

AS THE STORY GOES

Dad could reel in a fish
with one hand

as the other
in one fluid motion
lit a cigarette
and slipped it between his lips

while one eye
made sure I wasn't drowning
and the other
admired a pair of passing ankles –

people don't believe me
when I tell them this –

these days
I am one of them.

UNCLE ABE PUTS IN AN APPEARANCE
AT A FAMILY GATHERING

He came
like a shadow
after so much fasting
but without thirst,
without hunger,
looking lived-in
but not over-weary.

Sure, his face
was wrinkled
and his breath
less bold, less steely,
than his gaze.

But this was him all right,
the cream to some of that
old photographic cheese,
drug-free and proud of it,
withered hands hard done by
but still worthy of a shake.

Don't know how he got there.
No car.
No cab.
Must have walked from some place.

But he came,
drawn by the pull of family,

with an old-time song,
a story, a memory, on his lips,
and that warmth, that radiance,
of looking like
so many other people in the room.

AMY

I won't pretend she didn't go to her grave
longing for one more shot at the
Atlantic City slot machines.
None of that putting your life in order for her,
her withered hand trembled for one last pull
of shiny silver handle, eyes challenged
the light to show her luscious fruit
on spinning tumblers, while her ears
listened over the groans of the woman
in the bed beside her to hear quarters
clanging in the tray below.
So people came to see her in the hospital,
but they didn't fall into place.
And nurses whispered, she's doing as
well as can be expected, but that was
just like coming up cherries, winning
nothing more than your money back.
No jackpot, not even when her brother Sid came
and she guessed his name first time.
And what was I thinking...luck runs out
when you're waiting for your luck to turn.
Like breathing...breath after breath after breath...
and then...no more coins.

THE COVE

So tiny,
it was just a wisp of sand,
a few scattered rocks,
and some off-course waves
that rippled in from time to time
to break up in white foam.

I found it by accident,
proclaimed it my own spot
for seeking solitude and beauty,
good for the flesh and the eye,
and personal besides.

I'd sit there for hours,
just thinking and staring,
sometimes staring at my own thoughts,
then staring so hard until I had none.

Peace directed my body to lie down
or dip toes or fingertips in water.
It had me stand,
resonate with sea-breeze through my hair
or pick up a shell
and toss it back where it came from.

I was no nature boy.
Nor was I passionate about
reverting to some primitive state.
But here was a teenage frame

from tousled hair
to feet in flip-flops.
With nothing to distract me,
I took on its responsibility.

THE MATHEMATICIAN IN THE NURSING HOME

Worn down by mathematics, they said.
Searching for prime numbers so huge.
not even the universe could accommodate,
let alone his brain.
Calculations split his spheres in two.
Forlorn wrong answers
drowned their sorrows in his ganglion.
It was finding that his
piece de resistance,
ten thousand characters long,
was actually divisible by thirty-seven
that finally set his mind to bursting.
And he thought thirteen was his unlucky number.
Turns out it was this other one.

SHE CAME OF AGE ON HIS WATCH

He protested mightily
but there was no getting away from it.
His wife was tied up with her job.
He had free time.
Their daughter needed bras.

He rummaged through his options:
stay put in the car,
wander the sporting goods section,
or take a seat in the lingerie department
and shut down his eyes.

There were things about women
that he figured his current knowledge
more than adequately covered.
He didn't need to know more.
Periods. Body hair.
And bras for the recently developed.
These were off limits
to his sensibilities, his comfort.

Ultimately, he stood at the edge
of all that lacy, fluffy underwear
while his daughter engaged an assistant,
and the two talked in low tones
that he took pleasure in not hearing.

Father and daughter walked out together,
he looking straight ahead,

she clutching her bag
like a bank robber's wad of cash.

"32A," she announced
as they reached the parking lot.
That wasn't the number of the lane
where his Toyota awaited.
He wanted it to be.

MOUNTAINTOPS

Mountaintops flush with snow.
No wind.
I pull my jacket around me,
listen for sounds
to emerge from the quiet.

Mountaintops blue in the sunlight.
Only the holly speaks up.
Words red as lipstick.

Mountaintops white-capped
above rocks like raised brows.
How striking the sight.
The chill in my bones is worth it.

Mountaintops,
impossibly high ice knobs,
well beyond their first snug Autumn sleep,
huge braced shoulders
lording it over the frozen river,
the deck of trees below.

Mountaintops like solid clouds,
in this weather,
the great-great grandfathers of scenery,
old and wise,
nothing escapes them.

Mountaintops,
I report like a subaltern,
with eyes wide as French windows
and just breath enough to breathe.

WHEN TWO ARMY BUDDIES MEET UP FOR FIREWORKS

Down by the lake,
we set off fireworks,
some loud as the bombs we heard
in the desert,
others fiery and brilliant in the sky
and yes, like the moments before
we heard those bombs.

We're back in the army a little,
though it's a small town
and you're visiting
from a nearby state.
I'm showing you
where my childhood ended.
So with fireworks and matches,
I attempt to start it up again.

We scatter ducks.
They remind us of a marketplace
after an explosion.
But nothing is killed here,
no bits of glass and metal,
penetrating flesh.
It's just powder
and ours is dry as it happens.

So where do we go from here:
look for jobs where there aren't any,

go back to school,
pick up on the women we pursued,
now married, a year or two already
into their proper lives.

Time is fine with the pyrotechnics
but its mission is to move along.
We're just thankful
there's some old fire left.
And, in the years to come,
the populace is safe.
This blaze will be too busy killing us.

IN THE TERRACES

There ought to be a terrace for everyone
jutting out, top floor, tall building
in a big, brightly lit city at night.

And a drink of something glowing red
in a glass with a stem thin as a goose neck,
one for themselves, one for the lover

who joins them, whispers some cliché
about two perfect views that sounds
as if it's never been spoken before,

while draped in evening dress or tuxedo,
with a voice soft and warm as flannel, and eyes
that sparkle incessantly like the moon-rippling river

or lamps that light the pathway in the park.
Forget mere food and shelter, ascetic requirements
when the aesthete is called for,

nothing less than the world's population
at the end of act one of a Noel Coward play,
leaving the others to their canapes and small talk,

leaving themselves if that's what it takes,
closing the glass doors behind them,
stepping out into the cool night air,

the only options - love and beauty and awe.
I can see that now...no I can't see it.
We're all gazing in the same direction.

MISS DECEMBER 1955

She's fetchingly posed in a red bikini,
Santa hat atop her head,
its white pompom
falling on her bare shoulder.
She passed away this past April
at the age of 83.
No December is safe
from the Decembers to come.

THE DROUGHT AND FARMER JOHN

If only the grackles, the cowbirds, tilled my fields,
the ones that, masked, raid the last of my sorry seeds.
Yes, there's great wealth in imagining.

I'm one of many: Farmer Roy, Farmer Claude,
there's even a Farmer Amy.
My silos are empty.
My wide acres are sadly sown.
I move wheels. I hammer posts.
I'm responsible for every task bar the weather.

Earth ripened and glowed like orchards once.
Scraps of hope remain, grown parched and wrinkled.
A long dry summer seizes my farm
and gives me nothing for it.
Ah, life is such a long nightmare
interspersed with dreams.
It's an empty space
continually raided, emptied.
The dirt in my hand knows
what I'm talking about.
I am its servant but it no longer
has work for me.

Another day, wide open, crammed, from fence to fence,
with absurd rows of nothingness.
I'm a farmer - make that a prisoner of earth -
like my scarecrow, a skeleton hung with clothes,
straw hastily patched together.

And, above me, shines a solar husbandry of light and heat.
If only clouds were my crop and, just by looking up,
I plowed the firmament.

FISH

Beware, fish scaled silver
in coppery twilight water,
who swivel dances
underneath my eyes.

There are anglers
on the opposite bank
who long to make a meal of you.

You fling yourself away.
Then reel your body
back to shallows.
Your mouth opens.
Throat gulps.
Gills flutter.
Quick tail swish,
you're gone again.

You've no particular beauty,
just shimmery style,
blithe unconcern,
a joyful ignorance
of where the hook is coming from.

No particular beauty
could not ask for more.

THE MOON IN THE TREE

At five o'clock,
the leafy oak relinquishes detail,
clings to its shape.

The sky behind
is thickening blue to black.
How long can the center hold?

Moon rises,
unseen at first,
but then, where
branch takes leave of trunk,
a yellow crescent shimmers.

Fresh waxing
but shine enough
to ensure the tree
will not be taken from me.

So new moon,
tree-cropped,
wan light fanning out
from elements to whole.

On any night,
more modest aims
inviting my approval.

THE DEAD WOMAN OF BAKER STREET

The cop discovers
her seated in her kitchen chair,
head drooped over,
hands draped at her sides.
Her coffee is half-drunk and curdled.
Her last cigarette is nothing but butt and ash.

She's been living in that same old house for years.
Never married. No family as far as anyone knows.
When the cop peered through the window,
she was already a week into the next life.

She's carried out on a stretcher.
From house to house,
the eyes of the neighbors are out in force.
None of them really knew her.
They called her a recluse
and left it that.

Now they wonder was it her heart.
And that leads to concern about their own hearts.
And could she have been murdered?
Could they be murdered?
Her corpse owes them the truth

ORDINARY HISTORY

These neighborhood houses are marked
with historical plaques,

people and dates from the 19th century mostly,
ordinary folk whose homes have defied the years.

As a kid, the history I delved into
was mostly kings and battles, beheadings

and cavalry charges. There was nothing
about streets and sidewalks, doors and windows,

roofs slanted to defy the buildup of snow.
And those names and dates happened elsewhere.

An ordinary family doctor wasn't responsible.
Nor was someone named Tobias. Or Nathaniel.

Rulers didn't live in weathered colonials.
They didn't paint their houses white.

Wars weren't decided on the path I take
or the front yard where I stop to chat

or the creaky veranda where the old woman sits
day after day with her black cat and her knitting.

Yet maybe there's really two histories.
The one in books, the one of who's reading them.

WHO'S WHO

In a New York restaurant
I'm waited on
by an out-of-work actor
while the cook
is a wannabe playwright
and the busboy directs plays
in his dreams.

The guy that cuts my hair
is a poet.
The New Yorker can't recognize
genius when they see it.
And the Uber driver's writing
the great American novel.
At least, he would be
if his work hours weren't so long.
As for this woman I'm dating…
she's strictly renaissance.
An actor, director, playwright,
poet, playwright, novelist,
that I met at a Duane Reade register.
She was the one
with the warm, engaging smile
who scanned my bar codes.

In the city,
I run into so many people
who are something other
than what they seem to be.

I buy coffee
from the next great rap star.
The most amazing of all undiscovered voices
belongs to the kebob guy
who parks on my block.

But then there's a cop
who's happy enough
just walking his beat.
He's lucky he's a cop.
Around here,
living out your dreams
could get a guy arrested.

NO WONDER

She kept the house clean.
It kept her alive.
She cooked and she knitted but otherwise...
there was no otherwise.

She spoke some rapid French,
some slow English.
And she kept a diary
that was mostly about weather
or which neighbors said hello to her
when she worked in her front garden.

It was a quiet life.
And in a small safe town,
therefore a small safe life.
And, surprisingly, one without regret.

There was never a case of
"Oh, to be young again."
Whatever age she was,
even the older white-haired ones,
suited her well.

She polished silver,
dusted the family photographs.
The parlor was centered by
the piano her mother played splendidly
and she, clumsily.

The television was of
the old console type.
She never watched it,
preferred to read her Gothic romances
in the evening.
But she did not imagine herself
in the role of the imperiled young heroine.
If there was an ancient
but kindly nurse in the story,
then that was her.

She did have friends,
women just like her,
the daughters that didn't marry,
never moved away,
and were, at least according to the houses
in families for generations,
the last one standing.

And she attended their funerals,
one by one,
as the people she really only ever talked to
took their final sicknesses with great grace
and faded from their kinfolks' history.

The last thing she ever did in her life
was to make the house look half-way presentable.
After all, strangers would be tramping through the place
wondering whether or not
they should buy.

She did all she could
to save them the worry of wondering.

NAME THAT BIRD

As enamored of the scenery as I am,
the bird flies toward the picture window,
strikes it with a loud thump,
drops to the ground, sits stunned
until its senses slowly return all the way
before flying off
with a skewed opinion of its eyesight.
It was a warbler with lots of yellow.
A Cape May, a Prairie, a Palm, a Magnolia:
even when unwittingly posing for me
some birds don't make it easy to identify them.
The fact is, that bird would have had to suffer
more than just a slight concussion for me to nail
down its type and, from there, its preferred habitat,
its range, its song, its feeding habits.
But then the poor creature would be dead,
not habituating, ranging, singing, or eating.
For now, it's out there somewhere
in the treetops, in the sky.
Its life owes a lot to my ignorance.

A WOMAN ON A DOORSTEP IN WINTER

It's a brave act
to stand on your front doorstep
at dawn.
No doubt about it,
for it's January
and the landscape before you
is stark, blanched,
more dead than alive.

You squeeze arms against chest
for warmth
in contrast to your naked gaze.
The countryside is weary like time.
Its stories are buried in snow
and can be read no more.

There are no footprints leading
to and from your dwelling.
The big-talkers, the unfaithful,
live in a wandering world.
They found it hard
to put down roots some place
when that anchor was a lie.

From the fauvist shimmer of a horizon,
rising wind brings onto you
the flailing ice of startled drifts.
Sun lightens, from where you stand and see,

the work being done
by scattered creatures and resilient trees.

Despite its failings,
you love the outdoors
like you wish you loved yourself.
Temperature's below freezing.
Hands burn with chill.
It's bitter out but in a good way.
Your own bitterness is not there yet.

WHEN IT HURT DEEP

The night my eyes
slid out of their
sockets like leeches,
drained my face pale.

And my fists twisted
in opposite directions
like I was strangling
an invisible bird.

And I moved mindlessly
through crowds
like a rabid dog
nipping at the heels of sheep.

Now that was the death
of someone close.
The rest is just picking
at scab scores.

AVERAGE GUYS MOVE IN ON THE ABOVE AVERAGE

We sat ourselves at the edge of
some uncommonly comely looks
while wine's vaporous brainwash
made its usual false claims
about our virility and wealth.

Sure we had the intellect
but it wasn't wanted there
so we camouflaged our unloveliness
in more of the same
and then even more of the same.

Liquor revived our confidence,
sipped from glasses thin as waists
and our newly found loud voices
bullied our way into the conversation,
recklessly and rudely.

Of course we didn't belong there.
A sudden hush like we'd just broken
a crystal vase came over all,
a kind of eeriness, as all heads turned
in our direction, gasped in unison.

It was obviously time to leave,
too drunk to be insulted, to feel deprived,
out into the street, muttering how
it couldn't matter less, until the next day
when mattering drew a deep breath, began anew.

SELF PORTRAIT

Yes. that's me alright
but my left hand is my right,
the mole has switched sides,
and my teeth are thoroughly confused
as to which ones contain filling.

I move one arm,
a simple enough motion,
but reflection refuses to do as I do.
No matter how I try to bring image to bear.
it disobeys me
with this infatuation with the very opposite.

Then I look at you
and you're no better.
Your sides are switched.
I'm weary of saying,
"My right, your left,"
a thousand times a day.

I find it better to live alone
in a house without mirrors.
I get a better sense of who I am.
Long life's too short for contradiction.

BEACH RESORT

Along the shoreline,
dusk turns the sand pink
and, pleased with itself,
stays around to blow wind buff enough
to tangle the hair of the lingerers.

Summer rolls the film
for the second feature –
bright lights in the taverns,
heavy branches in the trees.

From behind a booth
painted like a clown's face,
a woman sells tickets to the carousel,
bright and traditional,
sixteen horses and two sleighs,
revolving to faux-calliope tunes.

Even as the bathers leave,
the surf keeps up its ebb and flow.
And, in the clubs,
young men and women
show off their glittery tans
but not their virtue.

It's the same every year,
only the people change.
Except for the woman
who mans the booth.
She only goes as far
as the carousel can take her.

THE GOLDFISH AND THE HOUSEWIFE

It exists in
the smallest utopia
on earth:

a castle,
some fake rocks,
enough water
for a ten second
circumnavigation;

on a regular basis,
God's fingers
dispense flakes
of food
that float down
into its open mouth;

it does not suffer,
never goes hungry,
and any unfilled desires
don't show through
the glass of its bowl;

you must pass by it
three hundred times a day;

your orbits parallel
but only touch
come feeding time.

HER PHYSICAL WORLD

She got up in the morning,
looked in the mirror,
swore to herself
that wrinkle
beneath her left eye
wasn't there the night before –
misquoting Donne,
any new blemish
diminishes me.

She scowled,
felt aggrieved,
angry at her body
for adhering too closely
to the rules of time,
as if her face wasn't aware
of all those wonder creams
she'd rubbed into its pores.

She wanted to cry
but that would only accentuate
that traitorous line
in her flesh.
Pale, it was bad enough
but red
and it would shine
like her drunkard husband's nose.

She made a vow
never to look into mirrors again,

to believe only what
her insides were telling her.
Unfortunately, they were
in town crier mode,
declaring her another day older
and with a brand new wrinkle to match.

But then the room lit up a little
as sun broke through a cloud.
It hadn't been a wrinkle at all,
merely a trick of shadow.
She felt no better.
What was a shadow
if not a foreshadowing.

THE GLACIER

It's a hundred feet thick of silence, of slowly moving stillness,
unbothered by the roar, titanic splash, where it caves in chilly bay
water.

I sit for hours on a boat deck as the liner glides ever closer,
nudging aside small bergs with

a sound like a feather pillow being punched.
Sun nibbles at the bright blue flanks, melts and strips, glitters in
the overhangs.

Brine eats away from below,
slowly swallowing blocks of floating ice.

Sun, glacier, sea - all exert the force
of what they are. My eyes are so meager.

I'm here for your sake. I travel to earth's ends because its
beginnings were so close, no narrow,
a lake for skating, lovers skimming the flakes of snow in dainty
figure eights.

I never knew the ice as such a massive, living thing, indomitable,
dramatic,
carving a path across a vast spread of landscape with such
unthinking obliteration.

I remember our life together -
so delicately designed, so gently powered.

And here - all is massive, unending.
But it lacks reflection. Maybe that's where I come in.

MAINE FARM GONE TO MEMORY

The abandoned farm
has not yet given up
its ghosts,
despite the weeds
sprinkled about the house's
rotting timbers
like graveyard-flowers,

Bobcats, coydogs,
foxes, whitetail deer,
that pan for food
in that multi-hued collar
of new wilderness,
still glance up occasionally
in case the old Maine farmer
steps out that unhinged
front door
in thick coat
and high leather boots.

The moose still probes
the broken kitchen window
for the old woman
whose bread smells
had been passed down
through generations
of wild things.

It will be many years
before these creatures understand
that man too
can be forced from his forest,
overtaken by forces
darker than fire,
more daunting than progress,

SWAMP FEVER

It's where the living
get to look dead.
Not just the sun-dew, the bladderwort,
the bald cypress,
but the green frog
stuck to its lily-pad
and the gator' scales,
a stalled log
in a clog of pitcher-plant.

The air is thick and low
like a funeral home curtain,
the surface baked brown
and rippling with turtle creep.

And the sounds are scattered,
a dollop from below
and then a shrill cry overhead.
Even in a quagmire,
lust and hunger must be heard.

A snake slithers across
the little land on offer.
The sheen of its scales
is muted by green-algae.
No need for it to bite.
The look of the thing
is venomous enough.

The swamp's a disease
masquerading as a landscape.
Natural chills, instinctive tremor –
I've caught it well enough.

QUICK CHANGE

Imagine pain that shoots from my head
clear to my ankles.

Along the boulevard,
imagination gravitates
from where cars splash white light
up and down the road
then rumble off into the darkness
to the dog that waits outside a bar
for a walk, for supper.

It's a once elegant neighborhood
that's now a realtor's bad dream.
On the overgrown sidewalk,
strangers try for darkness or light
but can only evoke a grayness
One has a face more bone than skin.
Another walks with his eyes closed like he's dead.
A third has enough teeth missing
for his tongue to poke through without bothering his jaw.

Some people lounge on stoops,
waiting for what or who I don't know.
Maybe it's for their legs to move.
They could be waiting there forever.
Imagine the kind of things some people
would be if they weren't people:
a stagnant pool, an amputated leg,
a gun against a temple
and a finger on the trigger.

And yet here's a young woman
with face smooth and brown.
She's curved like a violin.
Even when my breath has that contented sound,
it's hard to resist temptation
Traffic lights cut across me like a sword.
My nerves are taut as banjo wire.
I smell perfume that only means one thing –
a neat vibrant face with a warm, soft voice.
Time to press fast forward, experience the denouement.

Imagine joy that shoots from my head
clear to my ankles

THE TYPICAL POET

I'm a typical poet.

I walk the woods
with a notepad and pen.

In elms and oaks,
I seek out
the aesthetics, the rhythm,
of language.

At the pond,
my ears are engaged
with sound symbolism, meter,
my imagination seeks
a meaning beyond
a pool of water
thick with aquatic plants.

Birds evoke emotive responses,
wildflowers bloom assonance and ambiguity,
even the furtive ground-level creatures
are furry agents of metonymy.

I'm a typical poet.

I'm out with friends
on a hike.

I'm the only one working.

KEEP UP THE GOOD WORK

So poets have taken over the word "love."
Does that surprise you?
They're the ones who most often speak out
on the feelings they value.
Were you expecting the answer
to be lawyers or firemen?
And if it takes on a patina of literary
then so what.
Who inspires more?
Romeo and Juliet
or your next door neighbors,
Dick and Robin?
But this has nothing to do
with classrooms and books.
It's a direct line between the poet
and what occupies his heart.
No great claim to the "aesthetic."
No effete nod to academia.
Just sublimation to emotion's
pantheism and abstractions.
its acceptances and rejections,
its needs and passions
at a particular place and time.
Why shouldn't we respond to modern life
by rejecting all but
the sensitive, the unconventional,
the rebellious, the romantic.
The world needs the word "love"
to be more frequent in human parlance.
So poets have taken it upon themselves.
Cops and truckers weren't getting it done

CAMPING IN BAXTER PARK

Day bows down before the fire's rise,
as the stream's run of water
goes from sight to merely sound,
and thick trunks sop up so much of the light
that fading sun has little brightness
left to glimmer eye and cheek,
as I first build, then participate in,
this on-going flame
enough to cook trout and bluefish,
as chirring crickets take up
the challenge of the breezy shadows,
birds return to roosts,
and raccoons test their courage
with nibbling raids on camp's edge,
while you slump against your backpack
and dinner sizzles in a pan,
the coals burn smokeless
and the conversation's
more sigh than sense,
and the tent flaps applaud gently
like they could not agree the more.

BEE AWARE

We dip down
into where
sun and flower
collaborate
to manufacture
nectar and pollen
so as to gather,
digest and absorb,
metabolize,
regurgitate and store.
And yes,
we buzz a little.
That's what you hear.
The honey in your ear.

THE COMPOSITION OF AN ANTI-WAR POEM

Looking down,
I stare aimlessly at a blank piece of paper,
and my fingers that boast
a cicatrix from a paper cut.
Look – a wound.
I got it in my muse's service.

So how does this relate
to Mel polishing his M16
in a desert bunker
or Carter huddled in the heat
of a Bradley IFV?

Rifle fire near midnight.
A roadside bomb striking
three cars ahead.
Truck jolting, swaying,
threatening to tip.
And I'm scribbling down
the first words that come
into my peace-loving head

Would they encourage me,
their sun-seared faces
grinning eagerly,
like they are counting on my pen
for a forget-me-not
in case they do not make it home?

Such a quiet place here.
No roar. No explosions..
The occasional curse but nothing like anguish.
And I stretch life and death to their metaphoric limit
but there's still no true likeness.

The art of war is not war.
For no battlefield encompasses all of us.
They struggle against all manner of enemies.
I take up arms against the serene.

ARTIST AND MODEL

He reorganized her nature
into free space,
each stroke fighting against the flatness
of the canvas.

His brushwork
upended structure,
physiognomy
until she was all this and more.

He captured the slant
of her cheek
in her mouth's fingerprint texture,
paralleled the principle of her eyes
in the very place where they were looking.
He did not allow
appearance to
run away with his truth.

Days later,
he put down his paints
and her eyes scoured the canvas.
Where am I? she asked

He shook his head.
How she saw herself
had never been part of the plan.

WAITING OUTSIDE THE BAR

Man came up to me Sunday,
said, you weren't the one I saw
drinking in the bar,
or slapping those kids about the head
or slamming the door behind you
with the good woman still inside the house
shaking like the walls
or driving that car so wild
you wrapped it around a tree.

Those aren't your bones
that healed in a hospital ten days, he added,
your legs that spent a year in therapy,
your ears that couldn't bear to hear
the spiel of one more collection agency,
your voice trying to explain your mind
to a bunch of local cops.

You're lucky you're a stranger,
he said, that you don't look in a mirror
and see me, that you don't limp
when you walk, shudder when you think,
get a throat so dry your feet are stumbling
to the bar without even asking your head its opinion.

Who are you anyhow, he asked,
and why am I talking to you.
Then he brushed by me like I wasn't even there,
like whatever was there
had it made or had.it coming.

CORFU

Distant mountains
lie barren and stony,
still as the dead.

Closer to the eye,
towering rock cliffs
come alive
with soaring peregrine falcons.

Among the almond and walnut trees,
lungs inhale and appreciate
air that sweeps in from the ocean,
salty and sharp.

Fresh water's not forgotten here.
It spurts from red and gray rocks,
clear and clean,
with no instructions bar sipping.

Myrtle grows thick and wild,
its flowers like spiders of snow.
A strawberry bush
overflows with fruit
and a battalion of
two-tailed pasha butterflies.

But the olive tree is king,
five centuries old in some places
and bent and arthritic to prove it.

Resilience, fertility and regeneration,
gnarled and twisted like a Van Gogh painting –
such is the pitted, ungainly trunk of life.

The sand dunes are my true asylum.
Salt marshes on one side,
lapping Mediterranean waves on the other.
I stroll between acres of creaking rustling bamboo
and foaming whitecaps.
A minor event
as cures often are to other people.

CRANNIES

Crannies, and the smell of treacle…
I mention them now, not because it's time,
but for the heavy dosage of rain that just fell
and the surfeit of frogs that appear like magic.

So yes, I sat in the saddle of the rusty tractor
and pretended it was a tank and I was driving it.
And I came home with a snake skin
and my mother near-fainted.
And the well had to be pumped.
And my cousins were older and meaner than I was
but I was lighter on my feet
and just a little quicker at being a coward
than they were at bullying.

Lizards slid up and down hand-rails.
School was boring except when it came to maps.
Or tales of invasions and furious battles.
The killings in Crimea got me through many a long day.

And I brooded over eggs until chicks hatched.
I promised myself that, someday, I would
know the meaning of every word in the dictionary.
I rode horses, fed slops to the pigs.
Even milked cows when I grew older.
I knew where every magpie and sparrow nested.
Loved the smell of seed, of hay,
of cow patties, in the barn.

And the way the sun found every crack,
set the dusty floor alight.

And I had a fear of butcher shops,
like the one where the butchers wore
red-stained black and white striped aprons
and a dead sow hung from the rafters.
I had little interest in the garden.
But loved the waving. slithery sorghum fields.
I learned to swim in the dam
after almost drowning twice.

I was amazed by the high-pitched sound
of my grandmother's voice,
calling me for dinner,
how it carried across the hills
and into the grove of mango trees.

The sudden thunder rolls frightened me
but not as much as they did the horses.
And I knew where to hide when hard work was required.
Like a cranny with the smell of treacle.
But I loved the rain.
Almost as much as the frogs did.

MY WIFE AND I AT THE SYMPHONY

Five women in the orchestra,
she counts them
like the conductor counts time.

Two violin, one cello,
one oboe, one bass clarinet.

She hears them together,
a generous polyphony
of all things true
to their own ambiguity.

Or as part of the whole,
more amazed than she should be
at the seamlessness.

But she hears each singly
like nagging thoughts late at night.

It's wonderful music
but never quite free
of who's playing it.

INSPIRATION

She said it wasn't my looks
but the job I didn't have.
At least, I had a grand in the bank.
That's when I blew five hundred bucks
on the complete works of Mozart.
And I indulged in the best dinner in town.
The conversation with myself wasn't world shaking
but the Steak Diane was tender
as a lover ought to be.
I left a big tip…well why not.
I saw a play.
I even went for drinks later
and the bar-flies and I
shot the breeze until the early hours.
I acted just like a guy with a real job would act
only I didn't have to get up in the morning.
Flat broke then,
all I could afford to do was write.
So I wrote a poem for her.
Not because of her looks
but because it was my job.

FIRE HOUSE

Abandoning the burning house, grab what you can.
Some clothes, a doll, letters, a laptop.
But what about the late-night sex, the kitchen
lit by morning, coffee boiling, stew simmering,
and the couch, soft as a hundred arms.
Laughs, not likely. Love, we can only hope.
And looking back, what do we have?
A house with no roof, no glass.
A house without summer, without language,
without birth, without the Rolling Stones.
It's a fortress for ash to bear up against
old newspaper, tossed beer-can.
A toothless old man will crawl into
the shadow of its remaining wall,
He'll have a flea-ridden dog
that sleeps by his side.
But we'll do the scratching,
we'll do the yelping.

GHOST TOWN

Every morning, sun creeps over
the remains of rooftops,
shines its rays along the dusty main street,
into spider-webbed windows of shuttered stores,
on broken glass, rusty street signs,
a tire-less car that's been parked for forty years.

Sun shimmers the outside of most things,
turns crumbing brick to gold,
gilds the smokeless chimneys,
illuminates the numbers on mailboxes,
the busted windows of the dwellings.

Sun even skims the surface of the stream
where kids swam or fished,
families picnicked,
men and women got drunk on believing
this life would go on forever.

Late afternoon, sun moves on,
the town assumes it's more familiar darkness.
Nightfall erases
what time is slowly razing.

SCRABBLE

We're playing Scrabble
at the kitchen table.
I move tiles around,
first with my mind,
then my fingers.

Gale sits opposite,
I associate cricket chirp,
traffic noise,
a distant dog bark,
with her concentration.

We seldom play games,
rarely place ourselves
in opposition to each other.

Usually we're like
words that form themselves
without intervention.
Not these consonant and vowels
we've dealt ourselves
that resist any combination
beyond a few meager points.

In life, we're triple letters scores,
triple words even,
not these modest efforts
like "fly" and "was" and "did"
slowly filling up the board.

By the time we're done,
one of us will have won.
I prefer it
when we start out winning.

BAD ACCIDENT ON ROUTE CEREBELLUM

Memories collide with thought
like cars coming from opposite directions,
both hugging the middle lane.

My head is a mangle
of nostalgia
and what do I do next.

Gale takes my hand
like some kind of rescue vehicle
but the crash occurred
where she can't see.

Besides, her older and younger self
are in the wreckage.
Could she bear to watch one live,
the other die?

EXPECTANT FATHER

He spoke to me of the trouble caused
by her projecting thighs and full face.
They made him sick to the gut
especially knowing he had a hand in it.

He pointed out how her stomach
had become a landscape
and her muscle mysteriously powerful
while her shoulders, even when slumped,

looked strong enough to bear up the world.
There were still occasional flashes
of what he called beauty but mostly
she'd become this dockworker,

too busy hauling to be herself.
Then he added that, despite this,
the baby was in the best of health.
Just not in a good place, that's all.

REMINISCING FOR ONE

A studio apartment.
Futon mattress on the floor.
Could we have lain there happy our entire lives?
No answer.
It was no bigger than a dog house.
"Woof woof," she says.
So much for narrative.
She's quite comfortable in a home
in a bed with a real mattress.
And yet...
remember the packing crates?
Tables, chairs,
their versatility was matched
only by their fishy smell.
Aroma, don't you get it?
She'd rather sleep.
Battery died near the Carlsbad Caverns.
Ballooning.
Really, my love,
I give you permission to remember.
She mutters something about how
brackish the sea was on that day,
and then rolls over.
Now I'm talking in the language
of road signs and she's just
closed her eyes around the address
that's been ours for the past ten years.
She's willing to sleep on it.
Good for her.

But I'm still out there
wondering how I'm going to
find a replacement battery
in the middle of the desert.
And I'm laughing.
And then I'm two hundred
three hundred feet above,
her trembling whisper of
"Do you think this is safe?"
It's not and that's the point.

JUNKYARD GIRL

It must have been the way
she slithered, the way her
hip bones clicked and clacked like castanets.
The eyes had a lot to do with it as well.
They swelled with moon-light
and jumped out of her sockets.
Then they were like hands held out to her.
Yes, she danced with her own eyes.

Down by the swamps, she was
more the swamps than all that
brown, diseased water, those
bowed-head, sucking cypresses.
She was all that croaking and hissing
and grunting and shrieking,
all the noises that never seemed
to come from any one animal
but from the whole rotting morass.
When she writhed and howled
at the edge of that wretched marsh,
she reeked of that same decay,
breathed in and out rabidly
like gators feeding.

And she was the junk-yards too,
the rusting flesh of road-deaths,
the fearsome dogs that licked her,
the rats she patted like cats.
Atop hills of crumpled metal,

she flung her shirt from her body
like unwanted skin,
spun and screamed
while her breasts burst away from her rib-cage
like animals sprung free from traps.

She was every barren place,
every forgotten place,
like in my heart so deep
she was my heart,
became the low cackle of terror
at the bottom of my laughter,
the dark blood that drips out with my tears.

NO LONGER FOR OUR AMUSEMENT

They razed the amusement park,
invited us all to trample on its bones.
We did. We amused ourselves.
Step after step, we ground
the good times into the dirt.

I souvenired a rubber spider
from the haunted house
so all was not lost.
That arachnid is buried
in an attic trunk.

The amusement park went bankrupt.
Too antiquated.
Rides older than kids' memories.
Just not thrilling enough.
And there were no buyers.
Good real estate going to waste.
Developers. Condos.
But, in between, a graveyard.
Looking up, eyes tracing an arc
where a Ferris wheel turned.
Or knees steady where once
they wobbled at the spinning.

Old school remodeled.
Old house painted a color
my family wouldn't have touched
with a ten-foot brush.

Old friends moved on.
Or just no longer friends.
Old movie house shuttered.
Old dance hall now the
rarely visited local history museum.
Old not necessarily new
but no longer old either.

Just demolished in its way.
With only a rubber spider
to remember it by.
And that spider's buried in a trunk.
Even if it spun webs,
they'd have no grip.

SNAKE IN THE WOODPILE

Tom's axe is quick
but the snake is quicker.
It uncoils
from a maze to a question mark
to a slither deeper into wood
while he takes one step backward.

Its body says fear and escape.
His resolve is that
there'll be no next time.

He thumps his weapon
hard against its new hiding place.
The reptile flees into the open
but Tom is fully armed by this,
pursues like one possessed.

Down comes that blade
across the snake's lithe back,
sends it careening in two pieces.
The head rises up
in one last gasp for air.
The tail whips frenziedly
for a second
then is still.

Tom stares down at the corpse.
The snake was no threat.
His bloodlust was unlike him.
He has killed a living thing
and gained nothing.

THE BULLET

It's in a rush because it has a flight to catch –
your leg.

It's not a long journey
but, one microsecond late,
and you walk right by –
it crashes into a wall.

Its destination is the sidewalk
and it can't get there,
if you don't buckle at the knee,
drop like an elevator,
crash onto the pavement.

Luckily for the bullet,
it makes it just in time.
But there's no more luck
beyond that.

HAITIAN FAIRY TALE

That's moonlight, she says.
It's trapped between the blinds
but she feels as if she's cupped it in her hands,
Outside, a soccer game breaks up.
The weary players, backs glistening,
gather around a flask of rum.
In the fading light,
she is no longer just a daughter
but the wish for a daughter.
A dream pushes through the swaying shadows
and the dusk turns the dirty streets into paradise.
This little one dangles from the neck of night
like a rabbit's foot.

It is a fairy tale.
I feel as if I'm part of the story in her head.
Drummers thump beneath the wind.
Birds fly calmly into their night sky cage,
Soldiers shuffle down the sidewalks,
rifles trembling on shoulders.
A woman grips the elbow of her lover,
drags him into a dark doorway.
My little girl peers out in fascination,
understudies life.

I've seen the children in the market place,
dozing in chairs, in between the errands they run
for a penny here, a penny there.
She is not that child,

The smell of bouillon,
the sizzle of fried banana,
wander like dogs into the room,
My wife picks up scattered toys
in the background, cursing the mess
that's followed us across the ocean,
She is not that child either,
This child is in the castle tower,
her gold hair hanging down,
She is in the strange bed
awaiting her troupe of cheery dwarves,
My wife and I are the couple
made barren by a witch,
She is the sleep
only a prince's kiss can wake.

A NEW HIVE

I have the queen in my hand.
The workers have no choice
but to follow.

They are each small
        but there is no each.
Only all together.

They cover me
in one curious swarm.

Where am I headed?
What am I doing
with their mistress?

I have a new hive built,
the crown jewel
with an abundance
of flowery gems.

Nature, instinct,
have not been made over,
merely postponed.

It's a clear day
in the heat of summer.
We will make honey soon enough.

A DAUGHTER STAYS OUT OVERNIGHT

Sunday dawn and there's been no word.

The night's anxiety
contracts into the morning's pain.

Birds waken long before the telephone.
First one, then all.
The sparrows in the eaves
ring loudest.

Sun streaks the floors
of all rooms facing it.
It doesn't concern itself
with who's missing,
whose needs are greater.

Her father looks out the window.
A cop car rolls by,
slows down but doesn't stop.

Bad news is clever that way.

LIFE WITH THE CRUSHER

Is he really the most narcissistic man
on the planet?
Your diary says so
and it hasn't lied to you yet.
You've seen him, bare-chested,
flexing muscles in the mirror.
His physique is all he's willing
to take responsibility for.

To him, his little family
is merely the result of a certain comic hopelessness
when you slept together that first time
and now have a mostly unwanted son.

He bullies the boy.
He bullies you.
And there is always much
you are afraid to tell him,
even simple things like you're tired
and want your sleep.
For you see the dark coming.
But he prefers the company
of his sweat, his nautilus machine,
even on your birthday
or the anniversary of when first you met.

You can't identify
with his weights, his pulleys.
And when you start to speak

of something that interests you
he acts like some officious autocorrect,
so you only say what he wants to hear.
Maybe you need to see a psychiatrist
but what could you say in your defense?
How unlucky you were to run into him that day?
How hooking up drunk in bars sells romance short?

The truth is, bad as it is,
this is still the best your life has ever been.
So what's next?
He berates you until you feel better about yourself?
He beats you until the pain goes away?
You merely hope for the best
These days, hoping is the best you can hope for.

GREEN MOUNTAINS

I hike in green mountains.
My mind is as refreshed
as my lungs.

What better to do
but wander
with an eye out for the trees,
an ear for the birds
and the crackle of brush,
where timid creatures live.

My boots snap twig,
clip-clap on rock.
Then I stop for a moment.
A breeze blows gently.
The trees rustle.
A bracing respite
when I've heard enough from me.

FRUITFUL AFFAIRS

She's educating me in exotic fruits.
Try the rambutan, she says,
though beware the soft spines.
Really, it tastes like a grape, she adds.
But so does a grape doesn't it?

She cuts the smooth-skinned
yellow abiu into two white-fleshed halves.
Have to eat it now, it goes bad quickly.
But how do I let my digestive system know this?
It's still trying to figure out the sapodilla.

The woman in my last relationship
always left out apples in a bowl.
I could hold one in my hand
and know everything there was to know about it.
But a longan is a stranger even when it tastes good.

So this is what it's come to.
I know people by tree, the plant, the vine.
I used to date a citrus fancier from Florida.
And the one from Atlanta, she was a real peach.
And nothing else besides.

So what's this new one thinking?
That I'll never meet another with a taste for casimiroa?
Or one who shows me how to eat rollinia with a spoon?
Love grows, is picked, is placed on my table.
The question's not where it comes from but is it good enough to eat.

THE SPEEDING WOMAN

She'll be dead in a week, a month.
She's driving herself toward the reaper,
foot hard on the accelerator, pills a-poppin'.

The rising sun is an illusion.
She's not barreling triumphant
toward the coming dawn.
That's the night before up ahead.

Go back in time that fast
and the equilibrium
is busted like a turkey's neck.

Super-flat and calling out to her...
it's that kind of road, that
kind of distance between
who she is and what she regrets.
Like listening to friends
who turned out to be mere acquaintances.

Now, the phone calls are no help.
The hugs don't work.
The doctor in the back seat was heaved
just before her boyfriend passenger.
Where's her pusher when she really needs him.

Engine racing, gas flaming...not to worry,
he's in the details with all her other devils.

FLAT

This far out in plains country,
maybe you see people, maybe you don't.
The sky's your nearest neighbor.

Hot and dry most times, rain when wanted
and unwanted, sometimes the thunderhead,
huge and black and threatening

like you're living next door to an angry God.
And tornadoes of course. Land this level,
nothing can stop them. Only prayer tries.

When someone dies, you go visit the family.
When they're not living well, you show up
at their door with stew.

Outside the ritual of planting and harvesting,
all you need remember is church on Sunday
and never leave a gate open.

Flat land, flat singing in the local choir,
flat broke in the down years,
flat out when work needs doing,

flat days sometimes, flat nights always,
and smart types on either coast
itching to take a rise out of you.

SHALL WE DANCE

In our heads,
we're Fred and Ginger,
me in top hat and tails,
she in sparkling evening gown,
and we dance elegantly
across the floor
like we're straight out
of one of those 30's **RKO** musicals.

To onlookers though,
we're the dancing hippos from "Fantasia,"
waddling in our tutus,
out of step and possibly out of our minds.

Oh well, Ginger,
wrong movie maybe,
but at least we're in the frame.

EMILY DICKINSON ET AL

I've been to Amherst.
I've seen Emily Dickinson's house.
I walked the streets she walked.
Looked around.
saw much of the same scenery
that framed her world
one hundred and fifty years ago.
From there, I drove south to Hartford
and the homes of Mark Twain
and Harriett Beecher Stowe.
I could have just plucked
their books off my shelf.
But those are handprints.
I wanted footsteps.

LENA'S STORY

I had no time for strangers' come-ons,
never woke next to some guy
I didn't know from Brad Pitt,
never carried a loser's baby
or sobbed when one left,
or took a razor to my wrist
on a Saturday night
when there was no one in the house but me.

No one ever called the cops to my place
for me being too loud or too quiet,
and I didn't ever suck up to some social worker
in a pathetic, teary voice
about a pathetic teary life
nor get on the phone to some talk show host
to talk shit about the state of the world.

I don't parade my bruises
because I've got none.
Or complain about my periods
because pain's never been the kind of thing
that gets me to open up.
Nor is alcohol for that matter.

Never said a word about
how some kisses left their lint behind,
and others, their drool,
nor how the dark of my mouth
is sacrosanct
and tongues enter at their own peril.

I'm not the confessing type
which is why I always wave priests away.
I just smoke another cigarette,
feel that warm coming slowly toward me
while I blow out more smoke
than a steam train.

But I do look pretty in a new dress.
That's as much as I'm ever going to tell you.

APART AND TOGETHER

On Sundays, my parents
obeyed their predilections,
she with her much-stained cookery book,
he with fishing tackle and a can of wriggly worms.

Peek through the kitchen window
and you'd have seen her in that bright red apron
checking the pressure cooker gauge.
Watch him from between the trees
and there he'd be, on the riverbank
baiting his hook.

Or she could be hunched over a countertop,
peeling carrots and potatoes.
Or his line might stretch from hand
to slow current.

In those days, the house was her work,
with or without her children in it.
But Sundays were special.
Perfunctory gave way to loving care.

His job was in some dye factory,
but he drew upon nature for his life.
He preferred the peace of greenery and water
to the mad caterwauling of machinery,
the barely muzzled violence of the men
he toiled beside.

She kept busy. He stayed sane.
Apron tight around her waist,
no fear the knife would slice her finger.
His day was a gentle breeze
like the ghost of the water,
and a trout or two in his basket.

My mother wiped stove sweat from her brow.
The fish were never smart enough to elude his trap.
Dinner was ready at six.
He was home by then.
So were we all.
This was the family that gathered at the dinner table.
This was the family I was born to leave.

THE TRUCK AND THE DEER

Why does instinct turn traitor in the dark?
The ground under hoof hardens from turf
to tarmac and yet intuition sends out no alarms.
Along comes an eighteen-wheeler,
bright lights followed by fender and tire after tire.
Something in the deer's head says, "Cross the highway."
"The grass is sweeter. The dandelions tastier."
The combustion engine, the roadway,
have been with us much longer than anyone living.
The faculties of animals have had all that time to catch up.
And yet the doe still darts out. The driver's brakes screech.
The collision is loud and terrifying.
The truck escapes with a dent but the creature
is tossed to the side of the road, stomach split open.
ribcage smashed, legs tangled like a log pile.
Tomorrow, the scavengers will move in,
crows and vultures picking at the choicest parts,
no shame, no guilt, merely survival from the other side.
Who knows where the truck-driver goes from here:
to a strange city with a heavy load
or back home after a week or more away.
Does he return to a dying wife?
Does he mention the hit, the roadkill,
how quickly, how surprising, the world caters to death?
Or is the chemo working?
For all her unintentional stumbling into harm's way,
does the cancer swerve and miss, and the scavengers go hun-
gry?
The coincidences, the happenstances, are out there.

And we make these constant crossings.
Not always in the same direction.
Not always at the same speed.

RITA

Last night, I dreamed of her again,
though she's been dead ten years.
Funny how it's my hand always on her
cheek, not in anger of course,

but alighting there, like a Monarch butterfly
cloaking its wings around a tree branch.
It's funny because she was the one
of the long journeys, of the migratory patterns,

while I dug myself in like the trees,
my roots short on love some times
but always long on being here.
And yet the dream has me with itchy feet,

no longer feeling part of my own scenery.
It wills me to some place between worlds,
with her lying on a bed, still and silent,
like she hasn't moved for years,

and me with the dust in my eyes and
the mud on my boots and the seawater
shaken loose from my ears,
me with all of the places she's been,

all the things she done, aching in my bones,
throbbing in my head, beating in my heart,
me knowing at last how her hands reach,
to feel a familiar cheek, to find somebody home.

A_DY'S DI_ER (Thema)

It's been A_DY'S DI_ER for as long as I can remember.
Someone stole the N's years ago
and the owner, whose name's not Andy anyhow.
never bothered to replace them.
It's a local place and only local people eat there.
And they fill in those blanks instinctively.

The building's the old railcar style,
long and silver and shiny
and built during the depression.
The customers are mostly
long and silver and shiny as well,
except for the unshaven chins.
And their depression never gets much beyond
politics and ball-games.

The menu is a chalkboard
that Carol, the waitress,
changes once a year or so.
And the cook is Roy,
his body as tattooed
as his culinary skills are limited.

I eat there sometimes,
when I get the urge for muddy coffee
and greasy eggs and bacon.
The food is cheap
and the conversation's rowdy.
It makes me think those missing N's

stand for nicety and newness
or neat and noncommittal.
I don't expect their reinstatement any time soon.

A BRISBANE MORNING

The morning begins with pins and needles
as the arm I've been lying on all night
quenches its Saharan thirst on my blood.

I hear the crackle of eggs frying,
bacon snapping to brittle attention,
and the pop of toast.

Sun reaches in to shake me awake
before my mother cries out from the kitchen,
"Breakfast!"

Like my arm, my head's been drained
by the departure of dreams.
So-called real life is sucked in by the vacuum.

My sisters' shrill tones
dart in and out of my father's gruff voice.
The TV blares though unattended.
No question this is the right house.
The usual chorus of kookaburras, lorries
and plain brown sparrows
informs me what country I'm in.

I'm already the classic introvert
according to the wise ones.
I prefer the word "observer".
Or the phrase "deep in thought."

But I kiss and hug
with the best of family members.
And I recognize love
when I share a table with it.

From the divine solitude of the bedroom,
I step out into the bright busyness of the kitchen.
The quiet is where I become myself
but it's the noise that provides the opportunity.

THE PRESSURE

Is it my fault
that my life spits out
these nouns and verbs and adjectives.
Not forgetting adverbs.
And punctuation.

Unlike Shylock,
cut me and you run
the risk of a sentence
splashing in your face.
Dig any deeper
and you could be wiping paragraphs
from your cheeks.

When I first dipped into books,
I didn't realize
they were more than just stories on paper.
They were drip-feeds.
Other people's conversations
were injections.
And everything they did,
they did in some way to me.

It's a quirk of birth I guess.
When she was pregnant,
my mother was scared by a sponge.
Or a set of encyclopedias.
Or a poet reading in the park.

And can I be blamed,
when the English language
gravitates to my head
and that mind of mine
can only hold so much at a time.
If I don't write,
my skull could explode.
If I don't write,
you'll be reading my brain matter.

FARMER'S THIRD SON

The wind has had enough of the barn being in its path apparently.
A few angry roundhouse punches smashed one red wall in.

And it sure had no pity on cows and horses.
It twisted their hay like spaghetti on a fork,

then tossed it out into the bitter cold night.
And what it couldn't starve, it threatened to freeze to death.

Cows bellowed, horses whinnied helplessly.
If that wasn't enough, it fisted up under the eaves,

and pulverized the roof until it broke free.
Then came rain, heavy and blinding.

The wind may have swirled like madness
but it was the pitiful creatures that cried and kicked in panic.

The farmer ran out of the house in high boots and dressing gown.
His young strapping sons followed. His wife stood out the door

shouting "Anything I can do."
The fields needed the rain, that was a fact,

but not this much, and not of such malevolence.
I have visions of that night, drenched, determined men

leading horse and cow to makeshift shelter.
I was three months in my mother's stomach

but I heard the orders given, obeyed,
felt the duty, the hoofs and hard breaths of the common need.

If wind ripped my sides, rain pelted my skin red raw,
I had no doubt how this family would react.

Grim-faced, they would have gone out in the worst of weather,
braved the rubble of the barn, and saved the cows and horses.

TIME-OUT

At the edge of ocean,
we're at our calmest.
Our bodies relax on shore
like our lives cannot.

Look at me,
head on pillow,
body stretched for sun,
reading a lightweight book
to tan my brain
not fill it.

And look at you,
dozing in umbrella shadow,
your toes passing sand
from one to the next
like it's a beach-ball.

That water is deep
and wild enough to drown us both.
Likewise, the life
where the beach ends
and civilization begins.

But it's a peaceful time
so why waste it.
Or it's a wasteful time
but what peace.

BRIEF EXPLANATION OF OFFICE WORK

For those who don't know
the meaning of work,
let me explain it to you.

The phone rings.
I answer it.
An envelope is dropped
on my desk.
I open it.
An email pops
into my inbox.
I reply.

It's a series of reactions
like when the doctor
taps your knee with a hammer
to test your reflexes.

In fact,
my lower leg
often responds
with an unforced kick
to various office stimuli.

It's a brave boss
who bends over
near my shoe.

ANNA'S LAST WALK

She walked the shoreline
far to the south of here
and felt the cool, salty scent of the ocean
on her skin.

Her breath was as calm as it was easy,
her footsteps teetered this way and that
and her arms swung at her sides.

She didn't turn to see what prints she'd left
nor look ahead at the rocks, the rotting pier.

She may have mouthed some words
but the slap of wave on sand
took them out of hearing.

This was the day before she died
according to the two or three friends with her.
They settled down to an afternoon of sun.
She just wandered off by herself.

That's the story they're telling.
There's no character in it
who's found slumped on the couch,
strap around her arm,
syringe half-buried in the carpet.

Maybe she overdosed on the ocean,
or the dunes, or simply the need to be alone.

According to them,
she didn't stick a needle in herself.
She wandered off into the distance.
She died from drifting out of sight.

FROM MY TEENAGE YEARS

until a great mess
of jelly-shaped
information and meaning
arrives at my doorstep
I'm going to flutter about
the house like
a seven-day butterfly
flapping my wings
loving my colors
in the mirror

until someone plunks
that sloppy heap of sense
into the hollows of my head
I'll flit from room to room
high on my floating

until I can't help
thinking about this
I won't give it
another thought

I'm staying insane
until a brain gets here

THE FALSE ROAD HOME

Am I really almost home
or is this a madman's journey,
a strange place
he thinks he recognizes.

But trees I never seen before
seem so familiar.
And the houses could have been plucked
straight from my memory
if my memory were a lie.

No footing
but strangers are exactly like
people I used to know.
Except for everything about them.

Any moment now
I'll be where I've always been
welcomed, warm and wanted.
Yes, I am W in the dictionary.
But I am wasted
on the map.

THE MOOD FOR IT

Saturday night,
black car crawls down the street,
tracing yellow lines
in the tar;
inside, a man in dark leather.
even darker shades;
a raven hops along the sidewalk,
stops short
for a glass glint in the dust;
houses all shuttered,
windows barred by moonlight,
a woman, in slinky black dress,
wraps around the pole
of a broken street lamp;
drain covers clang
to passing footsteps;
smoke oozes up
from the tunnels of fire;
trash slaps against an iron fence;
chilly wind is the fabric,
an abandoned house wears it;

so many components,
so little effort on any part
needed to make a mood;
murky bar, gloomy diner,
the list goes on and on;
the cop's a clay figure,
the drunk can't be heard,

the scattered stores
are out of everything
but empty windows;

stay here long enough
and the soul takes on
the eyes of a dead man,
the heart of a stranger;
"hey you," whispers someone
out of the shadows;
if I don't leave soon
then "hey you'"s my name.

TWO YEARS LATER

Your ex-wife has a new husband.
Washington DC is still the US capital
so some things haven't changed.
But another slips in beside
that oh so familiar shape each night.
Hands you may have shaken once
cup her breasts, drift down between her thighs.
And when your daughter cries at night;
you only wake up on law-sanctioned weekends.
Every other three a.m., it's his eyes that part-open.,
that see the fog of woman rising from the sheets,
slip into the next room for some
rocking, whispering and soothing.

She makes his coffee in the morning.
He kisses her cheek. She hugs him back.
They look in on the child together.
He has your old happiness down pat.

THE BOYHOOD TRAIL

The trail never changes,
still snakes between
highbush blueberry and rock,
climbs hills, crosses fields,
returns to where it begins.

Viburnum mist cloaks the way ahead
but the crunch of my footsteps
on last year's leaves
is all the navigation I need.

On each side, firs compete with oaks
to see who can block the most sun.
For a time at least, the deciduous triumph
over the tall green lords of winter.

I find the pond where I once scooped up tadpoles,
run my fingers down the deep furrowed bark of white ash,
listen to the caw of the unwelcoming crows
and the piping curiosity of chickadees.
All is as before.
A forest is memory outside the head.

WASHINGTON SQUARE

I stroll through the cement park,
city above, glistening torsos below,
where skirts and shirts are flapping in modest breeze
and some guy is trying to sell me a wristwatch.

A fountain pours lightly,
smiles and rubs its chin,
while everyone in its vicinity
takes great pleasure in themselves.

My eye is an Italian director,
Fellini, most likely,
seeking setting, plot. characters
for my next film:

the Puerto Rican dancers,
a sidewalk painter,
posters for a hip-hop concert,
young girls dancing to a blaster's beat.

I buy a hotdog from a vendor,
for the thrill of mustard
dripping down my fingers,
as I loiter by the chess players,

and two yapping pooches.
An old bearded guy preaches communism
to a small crowd.
Another mutters poetry to himself.

Then the most beautiful woman
in the world
walks briefly into view
and is gone forever.

Well maybe she does
and maybe she doesn't.
But there's always a place for her
in my picture.

THAT BODY ON THE RAILROAD TRACKS

I heard later that the ambulance men
didn't so much lift the body as pick up the pieces.
One said it was easier this way,
like it was more jigsaw than real person.
Who else gets paid to put a puzzle together?

His buddy though said there was blood everywhere,
on the track, on the tips of the grass, on the rocks.
Every time he saw a train after that,
it reminded him of a razor opening a man's vein.

They both developed this habit
of just sitting some place and staring at people,
ordinary people, seeing how their bodies fit together, how they moved.
They didn't have to know them.
In fact, they were afraid to know them.

The first guy barely recognized
he drank more from then on.
The second guy though
launched himself into full scale depression.

The first was seeing a doctor for impotency.
He figured it was just the whiskey.
The other was in hospital for months.
They said he couldn't kiss his wife
for fear of knocking her down with his cow catcher,
slicing her under his hot steel wheels.

SUN GOES DOWN ON SULTRY SUMMER DAY

Crickets same-note same-place chattering,
cicadas clinging and clicking in trees,
mosquitoes so slow I kill more than bite me –
I'm never alone on the porch…
even the summer swelter feels like unwanted company,
along with the heavy clouds,
and the starling flock in temporary roost on power lines,
as dusk rolls in without enthusiasm.

Minutes pass begrudgingly,
thick air wishes time would stop,
insects infuse the humidity
with their surge of tuneless sound.

Early evening is when laziness feels most like death,
the shy moon emerges with little but darkness to wear.

I'm sure I'm not the only one unraveling at this hour,
not in this neighborhood of tightly-wound houses,
the streets of sameness, so many home-owners
locked into this desperate relaxation,
sweating, breathing heavy, as unlively as gravity,
crickets, cicadas, mosquitoes and people –
same lethargy, different life-spans.

THE HARDSHIP OF DOWNSIZING

It was a sad day
when I tossed those precious volumes out.
I believe I understood
what they were trying to say.
If not, it's too late now.
There were facts.
There was sensuality. And ideas.
And long descriptive passages
that took me places
with nothing but words for transportation.

And the authors came from all over:
Europe and America mostly,
but some from my home country of Australia
and the odd one or two from Asia or Africa.
Most writers were white men.
But there were women in there also.
And some black, some Indian, some Spanish.
I must admit most of the names above the titles
came with obits
but a few are still living.
and some have passed away since
I consumed their work.

But I'm downsizing
and something has to go.
Mostly everything.
I must trust to my memory
and the few books I couldn't
bear to part with.

Same with the music.
Same with the videos.
Same with the shoes
though I assure you
they're not in the same category
as these others.

And, I confess,
"War And Peace" went to the dumpster
with all my promises of getting to it someday
broken with one simple act.
But my wife has read it.
And I'm holding onto her.

BEYOND THE ARGUMENT

Sometimes, dimensions move.
Sea steals a row of pebbles;
hauls them off to deep water.
The bridge that stood so perfect,
glowing like a ship at dock
in the bay at night,
has no answer to fog.
Our windows do not always free
this looking, sometimes lie to it
harsher than love.
But we are calm now.
The air is among us
not between us.
It is as it was,
as it's always been,
like the first night in this house,
when we couldn't believe
where we were.
Your hand even rolls up into mine,
fingers exploring the battlefield.
And we both agree
that enemy,
since departed,
churlish and vile
with its fact right
and its feelings wrong,
is no friend of ours.
And these voices roll clean as tides,
do not flinch,

do not rise like king waves.
We're not curious as to the stones
or the bridge
as we stand side by side,
sentries to our marriage,
accept the fact that
boundaries must move, step aside,
to compensate
when nothing changes.

DELIVERIES

In my childhood,
the baker came by in his van,
the lovely warm smell
of fresh-baked bread
on our doorstep
as much a part of morning
as the sun.
I woke to the clink of milk bottles,
or sometimes even soft drinks,
flavors like pineapple or tangerine
that you couldn't find in ordinary grocery stores.
And, if that didn't get me out of bed,
there was always the thump of a newspaper
on our front lawn.
The mailman made his rounds twice a day,
even blew his whistle if there
was something in our box.
And, one time, when I was
in the midst of a virulent asthma attack,
the doctor even showed up at our house,
gave me a needle
to talk sense into my air-passages.
In summer,
the ice-cream truck
dangled goodies in front of my face
to the tune of Greensleeves.

My mother even reminisced about the ice-man
rushing up the front stairs with blocks of ice in tongs.

And the peddler on his bicycle, selling fancy cloths.
Life seemed less convenient then
and yet the day had barely begun
and we already had most everything we needed.
Of course, these all are ancient history.
Only memory still delivers daily.

A VOICE FROM AFAR

Last night, in sleep, I heard my father speak.

"Sorry I was never there for you, kid.
I left you in a house full of women.
No wonder you still can't change a tire
or catch a fish or hammer a nail in straight.
But that kind of living arrangement sure did
turn you into a sensitive son-of-a-bitch.
No wonder you write poetry.
I would have too if I'd have been
raised like you.
But you took to sports,
so that was always in your favor.
And you didn't let them baby you.
Well, not so much.
But what can you expect when you're
the youngest and the only male.
Jesus, even the cat was female.
It's an unpredictable world, sure enough.
I never planned on dying when I did.
I figured you'd grow up to be some likeness
of me — okay so maybe no mustache.
But I saw you as a drinking man,
a hard worker, maybe on the railways like me.
And you'd have a wife and kids.
And you'd stick around for them
just like I planned to do.
So here's me saying sorry
because I wasn't looking

when that train hurtled down the track.
And your life has been no ordinary life
because of that.
You live ten thousand miles away
from home for a start.
You married a foreigner in a foreign land.
And you still write that poetry,
At your age. Weird, huh?"

Last night, in sleep, I heard my father speak.
I heard none of the above.
I barely recognized his voice.
But my own is inescapable.

THE ONE WITH THE HAIR

She had so much hair,
like she was hiding in it,
the way it covered
half her face.
And the sheer length of it...
when her hair
sprayed across her shoulders,
its journey was hardly
a quarter done.

McDonalds wouldn't hire
her, she said, because
she refused to tie it up
above her head.
Same with the assembly line.
No net big enough for
that effusion.
Couldn't be a nurse
for fear she'd suffocate
her patients.
Or even drive a cab
with that hair
wedged between the door.

All she could do was be a lover,
lie across my shoulder in the dark,
flooding my chest, my chin, my groin,
with velvet, all smelling of Chamomile.
Best days of my life.
She had so much hair
it was just enough.

MISTAKEN IDENTITY

They were just walking
to the grocery store
when shots rang out.
That this could be
the last night of their lives
never once entered
their two heads.

They hit the ground
then lay there
as a window shattered overhead
and a bullet pinged
off the sidewalk.

"Are you okay," he said.
She was shaking
the sweat loose
from her brow
and didn't answer.

They set out
figuring they'd
stock up on enough supplies
to last the coming week.

Instead, their psyches took on board
enough dread, enough fear,
to last a lifetime.

It turns out the shooter
mistook them for someone else.

When they set out that night
for the grocery store,
they were themselves
and accepted the fact
that everyone in their circle
knew that.

But there was a shooter in the area.
Who they were was not nearly enough.

REGARDING MY TIME SPENT IN THE CHOIR

I was a solo tenor
every night
but for Wednesday practice,
all in preparation for Sunday
when I'd be one
of many voices.

My wife understood that
the sounds she heard
emanating from the bedroom
on a Monday or a Friday
were merely a part
of the whole,
should not be judged
by themselves alone.
In other words,
she didn't complain
if I strayed off-key.

She was in the pew on Sunday
listening to the choir,
immersed herself in the massed incantation,
thankfully unable to differentiate
my voice from these others.

No doubt, she loves me for myself
but there are times when

she loves me for how I blend in,
become indistinguishable.

It's not up to me
to know which is which.
I defer to my needs.
That's why I can't help singing.

Acknowledgements:

A Brisbane Morning: Willard And Maple

A Daughter Stays Out Overnight: Freshwater Literary Review

A Man Of Secrets: Orbis

A New Hive: Third Wednesday

A Phantom Visit: Muse

A Voice From Afar: IO Literary Journal

A Woman On A Doorstep In Winter: Straylight

A_dy's Di_ER: Thema

Amy: Connecticut River Review

Anna's Last Walk: Sandy River Review

Apart And Together: Havick

Artist And Model: Euphony

As The Story Goes: Mudfish

Average Guys Move In On The Above Average: High Plains Register

Bad Accident On Route Cerebellum: Press Pause

Beach Resort: The Phoenix

Bee Aware: Eno

Beyond The Argument: Frontera

Brief Explanation Of Office Work: Nerve Cowboy

Camping In Baxter Park: Eno

Colorado, May 1993: The Kerf

Corfu: Big Windows Review

Crannies: Art Post

Deliveries: The Broken Spine

Emily Dickinson Et Al: Abbey

Expectant Father: Rise

Farmer's Third Son: Verdad

Fire House: Wordfest Anthology
Fish: Zeit/Haus
Flat: Clackamas Literary Review
From My Teenage Years: Pinyon
Fruitful Affairs: Seems
Ghost Town: Third Wednesday
Green Mountains: Seems
Haitian Fairy Tale: Visions International
Her Physical World: Aura Review
In Search Of Edgar Allan Poe: I-70 Review
In The Hour Before Sunset: North Dakota Quarterly
Inspiration: Us1 Worksheets
Junkyard Girl: Slipstream
Keep Up The Good Work: Aji
Lena's Story: Havick
Life With The Crusher: De La Mancha
Maine Farm Gone To Memory: Nightsun
Miss December 1955: Creosote
Mistaken Identity: Floyd County Moonshine
Mountaintops: The Aurorean
My Wife And I At The Symphony: The Avenue
Name That Bird: The Tau
No Longer For Our Amusement: Slab
No Wonder: Red Coyote
Odd Habits: Third Wednesday
On Our Last Night Together, She Told Me This: Cold Mountain Review
On The Terraces: Round Table Literary Journal
Ordinary History: Coe Review
Psychiatrists At A Party: Orbis
Quick Change: Crux
Regarding My Time Spent In The Choir: Evening Street Review
Reminiscing For One: Jelly Bucket

Reporting To The Fishbowl: Haight-Ashbury Literary Journal
Rita: Exquisite Reaction
Scrabble: Picture Show Press
Self Portrait: High Plains Register
Shall We Dance: Bare Root Review
She Came Of Age On His Watch: Soundings East
Snake In The Woodpile: Slab
Sun Goes Down On Sultry Summer Day: Floyd County Moonshine
Swamp Fever: Oracle Fine Arts Review
That Body On The Railroad Tracks   Floyd County Moonshine
The Boyhood Trail: Birmingham Arts Journal
The Bullet: Slab
The Circus Was In Town: Talking River Review
The Composition Of An Anti-War Poem   Edison Literary Review
The Cove: Steam Ticket
The Dead Woman Of Baker Street: Coe Review
The Drought And Farmer John: Zeit/Haus
The False Road Home: Call Me
The Glacier: Chaffey Review
The Goldfish And The Housewife: Aura Review
The Hardship Of Downsizing: Qwerty
The Mathematician In The Nursing Home: Silkworm
The Mood For It: Call Me
The Moon In The Tree: Zeit/Haus
The One With The Hair: The Blotter
The Pressure: Soal
The Speeding Woman: Beside The Point
The Truck And The Deer: Havick
The Typical Poet: Abbey
Time-Out: Creosote
Two Years Later: Anatomy

Uncle Abe Puts In An Appearance At A Family Gathering:
Dunes Review
Village Life: Mad Swirl
Waiting Outside The Bar: Hubbub
Washington Square: The Alembic
What Sets Us Off: Lunaris
When It Hurt Deep: Penumbra
When Two Army Buddies Meet Up For Fireworks: Naugatuck
River Review
Who's Who: Plainsongs

www.ingramcontent.com/pod-product-compliance
Lightning Source LLC
Chambersburg PA
CBHW051832130726
47987CB00002B/509